ACID WESTERN

Robert Balun

the operating system
brooklyn & worldwide
c. 2021

the operating system
{unlimited editions} print//document

ACID WESTERN

ISBN: 978-1-946031-79-2
Library of Congress Control Number: 2020930888
copyright © 2021 by Robert Balun
edited and designed by Elæ Moss, Constantine Jones, and Robert Balun using the Operating System Open Design Protocol
cover art & typography design by Elæ Moss

 is released under a Creative Commons CC-BY-NC-ND (Attribution, Non Commercial, No Derivatives) License: its reproduction is encouraged for those who otherwise could not afford its purchase in the case of academic, personal, and other creative usage from which no profit will accrue.

Complete rules and restrictions are available at:
http://creativecommons.org/licenses/by-nc-nd/3.0/

As of 2020 all titles are available for donation-only download via our Open Access Library: www.theoperatingsystem.org/os-open-access-community-publications-library/

The Operating System is a member of the **Radical Open Access Collective**, a community of scholar-led, not-for-profit presses, journals and other open access projects. Now consisting of 40 members, we promote a progressive vision for open publishing in the humanities and social sciences. *Learn more at:* http://radicaloa.disruptivemedia.org.uk/about/

This text was set in 04b, Minion, Minipax, Freight Sans, and OCR-A Standard.
Minipax is an Open Source typeface designed by Raphaël Ronot inspired by the novel 1984. You can find it, and many more (as we do) on the Libre/Open Source Foundry VELVETYNE.

Cover image: The cover image uses an aerial photo of the California Aqueduct at the Interstate 205 crossing by Ian Kluft, via Creative Commons/wikimedia. Seen here is a close crop of the dual, mirrored paths of the aqueduct system moving through the state's dangerously dry farmland grid, textured and colorized in super saturated tones suggesting an altered, dystopic retro-future, with the title and author's name in 04b, a chunky typeface reminiscent of pixelated retro video game text.

Books from The Operating System are distributed to the trade by via Ingram, with additional production by Spencer Printing, in Honesdale, PA, in the USA.

Your support makes our publications, platform and programs possible! We <3 You.

the operating system
brooklyn & worldwide
www.theoperatingsystem.org

ACID WESTERN

ROBERT BALUN

‹CONTENTS›

AFTERIMAGE / 7
FELL / 19
GALLERY / 20
WHERE / 21
HIDING PLACE / 22
AMBIENT FIELD / 23
WHEN / 24
DESERT / 25
CYBERNETIC / 26
ACID WESTERN / 39

BACKMATTER / 60

AFTERIMAGE

fell through the portal into

all this this

it's easy to disappear

here or there

I don't remember exactly

I eat the dream

years

shimmer

away

molten time seeping

from

each being

I don't remember exactly

passing through

the mountains of cloud

a derelict spacecraft

inertia

all day

spent

looking in the stone corners

pulling up the shadow

to get at the time beneath

to try to keep

the name
that drips
from a mouth

in deltas

of cloud and nebulae

heat and sweat

atmosphered

a rippled through

memory

of the prism of self

slipping to spectrum

as light

sinks through leaves

drifting in matters of sun and season

looking for futures in the expanse

of who I meant to claim to be

in the architecture

of the event unfolding

its dimensional phase space

the house made of dawn

stormed dusk

collapsing

into refracted skylines

into a name that slips

into history

you can still hear the music inside

pealing

the sun

the excavated legacy

the prayers to

the sovereign ego

in the static of

the live-in deserts

the twelve thousand year present's

eyeball grind

weird rain

mutagen

truck routes

flight paths—

the loop
in the
loop in
the loop

of the making of the making of

disaster into spectacle

into the fine edge of a day

the house made of spin and spit

centuries dust

a goddamn

it's me
like a gameshow

the morning program runs

iterates

into the next
next

into the melted

into the wake up
subroutine

wake up
look for traps

what banners will come to cover me

what therapeutic pennies

what taken your hair and hexed it

what portal

what void

what umber decades

scattered in atmosphere

what you

what me

in the dispatches' days' years' of

unstable

the fragility of moments

hewn

quantum

low-bent

in the ambient
here

each

being

passing

through

each

being

slips

you fragment into you

a song dissolved in the dawn

FELL

through the portal

into all this this

I don't remember

exactly

the rest of the beginning

GALLERY

I keep seeing you

walking through

the elusive

operating

oscillating

facets
of time

left in the noise of
just
now's

reverberating

visage

glown
in a frequency
attuned to

a brittle

crystalline I

WHERE

I drink the cough syrup

where I can't take the day off of work

where I get paid by the hourly contingency
a contingent

where my heart races to seemingly almost
bursting

where I drink water from the same
cup as I water the plants with

where I say hello to my spider friends

where
tomorrow
maybe

you'll find someplace soft to rest for awhile

HIDING PLACE

here is not a place of honor

all of that for this

a hiding
for the fires of the dream to oxidate

which doesn't mean
the world ceases
to fall apart

but maybe if you
unspool a logic

there will be a reason

for this rendering of thorn

a requirement we can't guarantee

the quick answer is that
we must build many more secrets

chambers that we hope to keep hidden from you

the last glow
of the energy of our time
spent here

maybe it's better to remember to forget forever

the question of value

of when you become

AMBIENT FIELD

in the time
spent

worshipping time

in the arranged

shipwreck
city

*

a whispering voice in the dark

hungers on

*

in all of this this

the penitent rush

serpent is lord

a banner so big the wind couldn't lift it

*

in the bones on the table

the wilderness of a vast organism

WHEN

       did we begin the performance of the day's

       pattern
       making

       spun in the gauzy vision of irradiated light selling your youth back to
       you

       unfolding it
       into day
       into day—

       the end of the map looks just like
       the beginning

       all of the equestrian statues in every city in the world assembled in
       the pantheon of triumphant tribunal avenues in the desert of the real

  DESERT

                                    we have emergencies
                                      we have bail bags

                                    we have chimerizations

                                    these were the years

                                                tell me
                                      what my name was

                                         I just wanted

                                      to touch my debt
                              hold the weight of its corpus
                                        across my back

                                         the lifetrap's

                                             montage
                                              data's

                                              world
                                             building

                                             melted

                                             memory
                                              dream

                                      chewing on my lips

                                      visions in the scrim

                                     the particle mandala

                                            collapsing

                                            to return

CYBERNETIC

*

fell

through

the portal

into all this
this

*

I can never remember
the rest of the beginning

*

gyred in

the looped

fragments of looping

*

information dissolves in atmosphere

breathing

*

these are secrets

*

the world kept

*

imbued in the shrapnel of the executed broadcast

*

the map slithers its shape

*

the city

liquid

drips through

time's melt
of old sunlight

*

the remnants and the relics

*

settled in cement

*

dressed up like

the bunker life

promised

*

kept

phase

shifted

*

in-
to
and
out
of

*

the shimmered

*

in
situ

*

my
abstract

*

data

*

extracted

strata

*

stare through the ads

★

try to remember shit

★

I see myself

from time to time

★

in the clacking
edifictic
static

★

the tremoring

★

dream

★

have you got your
papers

★

otherwise they

won't let you in

★

kept

*

strangers

in the body

*

here is not a place of honor

*

someone tells the story

to stay afloat

*

sustained
sustenance

*

waxy

skin

and toxic

*

the territory of mutation

*

looking for the edge of this this

*

movement's

searching

motion

*

logged
in the ledger's

surveillant

workfare

*

correlated and captured

*

for participation in the

*

what are the details of your model

*

the game score
of your past and

predicted future

*

of someone who might
look like you

*

a fly in your ear

*

kept close

*

the body

aches in

the pace

*

deployed in the privatized
individual

*

of consensual sentiment

*

find more hours

*

right

*

the perpetual present

*

the looped fragments of looping

*

taught to

scatter

through it

*

my smoke hole

pluming

*

to be burned
fast and bright

*

who was there

*

who

machines

each being

*

put to

*

a pocket full of wires

a bucket full of teeth

*

an object

made to be

*

as you

*

the turbulence of air

*

as you

*

move
through
the viscous
atmosphere

*

revenants
performing
function

*

the ground sparkles with stolen gold

*

told
as spoken voids

*

cut from

*

scraps and citations

*

performing

*

the psychic pollution

economy

*

memory

*

dream

*

landscape

*

speech

*

a medium
offered

*

allowed
to be

*

summoned

*

from time
to time

*

in the dialectic of apocalypse

*

by the automated fetish gods

*

in the control key

circuit
origin
myth

★

who is allowed to be who we will become to be who will build what we will be

★

ACID WESTERN

fell
through

the portal

into all
this

shadow

I can never

remember

the rest of the beginning

the memories I

keep

operating here

in the twelve thousand year

mesopatamian

agrilogistic

coding history

all these years
we've been

collapsing

in the looped
fragments

of looping

the morning

program runs

the fumes

make

me

light

excuse me

is today

wednesday

I keep

walking through
the elusive

a frequency

attuned to

the certified window

the glass coin

machine in your station

all droney
noise and light

please
come home again

every day is
permeable skin

      is
documentation

      is
gravity

      is

I

keep thinking I

see you
walking by

in the wandering

in the

but I forget
many times

I sit around and wait for good news

my yellow grows
along my hands and chest

save your money and die

is that where I live

everything sparkles when you fill your head with glass

light dripping from your fingers

I wander around the front yard

the houses filled with stones

the morning program runs

the looped
fragments
of looping

excuse me

is today
wednesday

I have been

made many substances

into and out of phase

timeline's friction

turns out
smoke

all that energy
and the day hasn't even
begun

the count's
figure's
ledger's

atmosphere

of slow disintegration

one
atom
at a time

body been

the smoke in my hair

the sports broadcast

the storefront
preacher

the echo in

the highway static

the promise of stasis

I forget

many times

excuse me

where have I been

when do I
wake up brand new

when will I
be made clean

I just keep asking for
everything

no personality only
an arm driven
by a mind that is absent

send your soul through the ringer
for the pennies I let leak into my mouth

a careless appetite

like a good assassin

time gets all fucked up

all the lights

crashed and scattered along the street

the smoke of a tenuous life in your lungs

ash on your sleeve

and only a little blood from the teeth today

I was thirsty

and died from thirst there

a leaky vessel

pushing through the space before it

the spectacular frame's

canyons of mist

a bright singing

chorus in the ambient

but I forget many times

the dream all day

the ambient here

my brain leaks decades

of sand

an ill-fitted suit

in the twelve-thousand year

mesopatamian

present

                                how far away
                                       am I

            what kind of money is in my pocket

                                  maybe this is
                                the hyperobject
                                   environment

                                      collapsing

                                            into
                                        my lungs

                    the geode of the haze rainbow's

                          spectrum of particulate

            shifting through the visions in the scrim

                                  was I anywhere
                                    in my shaky
                                    recollection

everything all at once

again and

another day of news and another

history's
rippling
entity

of past unfolding

the incomplete present

I forget

the rest of the beginning

light keeps shifting to
the same mornings I

forget exactly I

flood my mouth with mutagen I

resolve sometimes in the I
kept in

synthetic
fragrance

and smoke

the ads stream by

the ads stare back I

resolve sometimes in

the angles of surveillance

extracted I

own no time

in the maze

blurred

microcosmic works

in the agrilogistics at the edge of vision

in the no place
in the only here

only the worn out heels

second-hand shirts

bodies in the bend

de facto
designed
to be lack

in the dissolving collapse

in the regimental medics
rummaged in your head

kept
phase
shifting

looped
fragments
of looping

in the privatization of stress

low bent

in the ambient

honey

drone

21st

century
centurion

the mirrored

photons

dripping
from
the eye

excuse me
is today
wednesday

the morning program runs

the dissolving collapse

drifting to
the future's

rendering of thorn

in the dream
in the dream

I am comfortable and clean

cleanly gated

I smell like a hotel room

a targeted

marketing
marked

neuro-
voider

in service of the static

dressed up like

the bunker life promised

the garbage scows drift by

but I forget

many times

in the end command

in the military parade of the everyday camouflage

in a facet of a map of infinity

inside the ruins
the programming

[   ] was here
and
[   ]
and
[   ]

and here

and here

we can't go home again

that's where they're building the ziggurat

who gets to be

someone

anymore

I keep thinking
I see you

in the uncanny everything

in the snuff of stale sweat and piss

in the heavy heat

in the hyperruin

the land of magical bullshit

secret kings and client states

dust
sun

pacing

the mythology

the time

gathered up and arranged here

inside the perfect standards of a pop song

inside the dissolving collapse

the problem of reality

here

where our lives intersect

ACKNOWLEDGEMENTS AND BIBLIOGRAPHY

Grateful love and acknowledgement to those who made this book possible.

Bianca for your luminous warmth, your unceasing pursuit of your creative practice, and for being as silly as I am

Mom, Dad, Jess, and Chris for always being there providing foundations, near and far

Michelle Valladares and David Groff for your generosity and support, in numerous ways, in shaping me as a poet, teacher, and person

Rozanne Gold for all of our work together at your kitchen table

Carlos Franco for all of the theoretical conversations, big and small

Josh Goulding for all of our talks and easy time, and for your dance moves

Marie Davy, Josh Hari, and Camille Moussard for all of the music and meals

Constantine Jones for always being up for discussing poetry and beyond, and for your help with this book, from notes, to draft, to galley

Elæ for all of your labor, not just on this book, but for building the visionary and radical process that is The Operating System

Many thanks to *decomP*, *Dream Pop Press*, *Ghost City Review*, *'Pider*, *Powder Keg Magazine*, and *Reality Beach* for publishing versions and excerpts of some of these poems.

In no particular order, an incomplete list of people and work I was reading, looking at, listening to, and thinking via:

Alejandra Pizarnik, Nicole Eisenman, Andrei Voznesensky, Kazim Ali, Tia Myles, Donald Dunbar (*Safe Word*), Nanni Balestrini (*Blackout*), *Into Eternity*, Terre Thaemlitz, Khruangbin, Reza Negarestani (*Cyclonopedia*), Florian Hecker, Ian Cheng, Timothy Morton (*Hyperobjects, The Ecological Thought, Dark Ecology*), Cinthia Marcelle, James Turrell, Nina Simone, Cymande, Hailu Mergia, William Tyler (*Modern Country*), Chaz Bundick Meets the Mattson 2, Chuck Johnson (*Balsams, Velvet Arc*), Peter Milne Greiner (*Lost City Hydrothermal Field*), Nayland Blake, Katharina Fritsch, Samara Golden, Laura Oldfield Ford (*Savage Messiah*), Hito Steyerl (*Duty Free Art*), Yuri Herrera (*Signs Preceding the End of the World*), Mark Fisher, Ida Börjel (*The Sabotage Manuals*), Leslie Kaplan (*Excess the Factory*), Chris Forsyth and the Solar Motel Band, Ursula K Le Guin (*Always Coming Home, The Dispossessed*), Shay Roselip, Graves (Greg Olin), *Another Green World*, *SMiLE*, SE Rogie, Huma Bhabha, Aase Berg (*Dark Matter, Hackers*),

AGRILOGISTIC LOOPS

A CONVERSATION WITH ROBERT BALUN

Greetings! Thank you for talking to us about your process today! Can you introduce yourself, in a way that you would choose?

Hello! I am honored and humbled to be in this space as a collaborator with The Operating System.

Why are you a poet/writer/artist?

Being a poet (which for me entails being an active reader as much as it does actual writing) is a means to think about and process the world around me, my place in it, particularly the privileges I have as a straight, white, male, working to mitigate the harm of those privileges, while beginning a dialogue with a reader, a literal point of connection, if asynchronously.

When did you decide you were a poet/writer/artist (and/or: do you feel comfortable calling yourself a poet/writer/artist, what other titles or affiliations do you prefer/feel are more accurate)?

At some point my writing practice became something more intrinsic, vocational, and this is when I felt comfortable and confident in that identification. But also, more importantly, I began to see being a poet as only one aspect of being in the world. Writing helped me to consider and inform who I was in the world, and that it was important for me to take on additional, constructive work. In my case, this work manifests itself in my teaching and in my work as a union organizer.

As a teacher, working in the classroom is a way to explore ideas and to apply literary study, working with students to practice revealing, understanding, and dismantling the obfuscated structures that dominate each of our lives, in different ways. The City University of New York university system is one of the largest and most diverse public university systems in the country. As a white professor in this space, it has been vital for me to consider my own position of privilege and how to be most effective towards, and supportive of, the needs of my students, trying to understand the issues that my students may be facing, issues that I by and large do not have to deal with, considering this in the development of curriculum that is potentially useful and relevant to their needs and validating to their experience. While each student's life and background will differ, part of my job as a teacher is to empower their perspective, to offer tools for students to engage with the world through their experiences, and to assert the validity and vitality of their voice through their writing and coursework. More structurally, I've done things like institute labor based grading contracts in my classes to help mitigate the so-called meritocracy of typical grading schema perpetuated by the neoliberal academy. As an adjunct, the primary issue that I run up against is economic precarity, but it's been important for me to understand and connect this to the issues my students might be facing, to link our struggles, though I do not experience the hierarchical violences of this country to the same degree that they might.

In addition to my work in the classroom, I found it important to get more directly involved in the issues confronting CUNY in general, specifically the racist austerity that undermines the quality of my student's learning conditions. This is why I volunteered to become a union delegate, to help shift the conversation and trajectory of the union. For example, the group of organizers that I caucus with, Rank and File Action, managed to help pass a resolution that explicitly calls for the union to begin strike preparation, something the leadership had resisted, even as CUNY faces cut after cut from Democratic Governor Andrew Cuomo.

Being a poet, then, has led me to these more active roles, and I'm grateful for the impetus.

What's a "poet" (or "writer" or "artist") anyway? What do you see as your cultural and social role (in the literary / artistic / creative community and beyond)?

Poetry led me from the internal to the external, to working more directly in the world, and for me that meant getting somewhat further afield than the literary community. I think working to be as collaborative and constructive as possible has been a general motivation in this regard, which is one reason that I came to The Operating System, first as a fan and then as a volunteer (more on this below).

Talk about the process or instinct to move these poems (or your work in general) as independent entities into a body of work. How and why did this happen? Have you had this intention for a while? What encouraged and/or confounded this (or a book, in general) coming together? Was it a struggle?

I've never really been able to sit down and write a poem. There's always some external thing that sets off a line of thinking that becomes a poem down the line. Plus I've worked 2-3 jobs at a time for the past 9 years so I don't have a tremendous amount of time anyway. As a result, I developed a practice of writing notes, lines, phrases, stanzas, on the move, usually while commuting, and then composing those into "standard" 1-2 page poems. These notes were usually pretty structured, as I was trying to make them into poems as I was writing them, a restrictive mistake, I think now.

At some point in the process of writing the poems that would become this collection, I realized all of these 1-2 page "poems" were part of a bigger sequence, and I began to get rid of their individual titles, I began to literally cut out the parts I liked best or thought were the most interesting and started to arrange them into the sequences they appear as in the book.

Putting together the collection in this way opened up my process and gave me permission to work differently. I stopped trying to write singular poems and I started writing the collection first, thinking of the collection as the object, instead of the individual poem.

Did you envision this collection as a collection or understand your process as writing or making specifically around a theme while the poems themselves were being written / the work was being made? How or how not?

About halfway through the process, I understood that I was writing a collection, which helped me see how everything I was writing fit together, or how it could fit together. Figuring out the title also helped cohere everything (more on that below).

What formal structures or other constrictive practices (if any) do you use in the creation of your work? Have certain teachers or instructive environments, or readings/writings/work of other creative people informed the way you work/write?

While completing my MFA at City College, Michelle Valladares and David Groff were immensely supportive in terms of their responses to my work. Even then (2011-2014), I was writing weird little poems that weren't particularly narrative, and Michelle and David both encouraged that experimentation in such a way that I began to feel comfortable in that mode. During this time, my friend Karin Olander was also fundamental to facilitating a sense of a poetics to pursue.

Less personally, the world-building in the work of Ursula K Le Guin and Jorge Luis Borges stands out as influential to the shape of the poems here.

In different ways, there seems to be a shimmering contour of strange yet familiar worlds in their works, and I wanted to attempt something similar in a collection of poetry.

More broadly, all of the musicians, artists, writers, thinkers that are listed in the "liner notes" portion of the acknowledgements page were all vital to the aesthetic texture of these poems, in some way. These poems don't exist without that resonance.

Timothy Morton's theory of agrilogistics was also important to thinking about this collection. Agrilogistics is the idea that agriculture is a kind of algorithm that has been upgrading itself since humans first began to cultivate plants and animals on a large scale, beginning in Mesopotamia (which is why those references pop up in the book). As agriculture continued to be optimized by humans, it continued to upgrade itself and mutated into different forms and resulted in new technologies and all sorts of things: writing, kings, aristocracy, etc., etc. The trajectory of human history, civilization, globalization, begins there, is an outcome of that, and that we're looping through, iterating through that original input. This quality of looping repetition that seems to dominate life in the 21st century United States/west is a primary concern of this book, how this country keeps replaying the same traumas and tragedies, of racist police brutality, cycles of poverty, repression and marginalization, played out on stolen Indigenous land in the ongoing legacies of settler colonialism.

Speaking of monikers, what does your title represent? How was it generated? Talk about the way you titled the book, and how your process of naming (individual pieces, sections, etc) influences you and/or colors your work specifically.

The acid western is a small sub-genre of western films that started being made in the 1960s, which are essentially anti-westerns, or countercultural westerns. When I came across the name I was immediately drawn to it as a title and thought that it could be a unifying concept for the poems I was working on.

The book isn't exactly a western in the sense of the typical genre, but the poems are concerned with the west in terms of capitalism and its entanglement with the repeating, reverberating myths of manifest destiny's justification for genocide and (North) American exceptionalism, which continue to influence the imaginary archetype of what it means to be "American" and the money-hustle-bootstrapping death cult and general worship of wealth we see in today's version of the United States; the perpetuation of those myths as a kind of iterative loop. So that would be the western part.

The acid part works on a few different frequencies:

-acid in the sense of the hallucinogenic, mutagenic, malleable, and collapsing ontologies and realities of each day spent in the 21st century west; and if the former are viewed as a description of a state of being, there is a sense of atemporality caused by that liminal state, in this case the looping repetition and effect of the day to day, whose essential character seems the same and fixed;

-in the sense of sharp-tongued critique;

-and lastly, in the sense of disintegrating and melting all that down to construct a just, inclusive and dignified place to be in the world.

What does this particular work represent to you as indicative of your method/ creative practice? your history? your mission/intentions/hopes/plans?

My hope is that this work will represent an articulation of a relatable and useful phenomenological impression of an epoch.

What does this book DO (as much as what it says or contains)?

The last line of the book in particular seeks to directly and literally connect to the reader. Through that connection, I hope to posit that the struggles for justice in the United States, and globally, particularly those that might be further afield from one's own experience, are a matter of collective action, and that the collective begins to be built one person at a time, connecting individual struggles to collective ones, caring about those that are not directly related to you. How does an idea translate into praxis out in the world? This is a question I want to prompt with the last line of the book.

What would be the best possible outcome for this book? What might it do in the world, and how will its presence as an object facilitate your creative role in your community and beyond? What are your hopes for this book, and for your practice?

I hope that this book will encourage readers to seek to understand the interconnection of the ongoing social (and ecological) violences being carried out, day after day, all over the world. I hope this book will be a point of resonance for readers that offers some clarity to move forward with; a point of connection that helps to facilitate the work of dismantling the violent and oppressive systems that dominate the lives of many.

Let's talk a little bit about the role of poetics and creative community in social and political activism, so present in our daily lives as we face the often sobering, sometimes dangerous realities of the Capitalocene. How does your process, practice, or work otherwise interface with these conditions?

The issues of time, information, and living paycheck-to-paycheck fundamentally inform the structure and content of the poems. Beyond that, as I hope I have conveyed, reading poetry, prose, and theory, alongside writing poetry, has been a way for me to seek to better understand not only the ruinous structures that manifest themselves in this world, but also my place and role within the perpetuation of those structures, working to mitigate those effects, working to undo these effects and those structures. The process of being a writer (and the work which that entails beyond just writing) has been a way for me to develop a knowledge base, with one project or line of research informing the next, to seek to always try to see and know more, to always try to be better out in the world.

I'd be curious to hear some of your thoughts on the challenges we face in speaking and publishing across lines of race, age, ability, class, privilege, social/cultural background, gender, sexuality (and other identifiers) within the community as well as creating and maintaining safe spaces, vs. the dangers of remaining and producing in isolated "silos" and/or disciplinary and/or institutional bounds?

Well, broadly, I would suggest that any system conceived under or within an oppressive system, such as publishing within capitalism, will by and large bolster and exacerbate the oppressions enabled, perpetuated, and profited from by that system--white dominated, patriarchal, heteronomrative, ableist, hierarchical, financially exclusive, opaque--a reflection of the systems in the United States and capitalism at large. How are these struggles addressed structurally, from the point of conception, of what it means to publish, either as a writer, editor, or publisher?

One reason I wanted to volunteer with The Operating System was because it directly challenges these systems of oppression in publishing and beyond. As a volunteer, it was possible to assist in a collaborative and significant way, working with authors and cohorts, working on initiatives at the OS that model an actually existing alternative to the exclusionary and capitalist microcosm of the publishing world, offering resources and community beyond just the book object for capitalist consumption, even more so now with the launch of Liminal Lab, providing additional means of collaborative and empowering support, a node in the network of solidarity. Looking inward to turn outward, how can I personally, given my context as a straight, white, male, help to facilitate that network?

ABOUT THE AUTHOR

Robert Balun is an adjunct professor at The City College of New York, where he teaches creative writing and literature. He is the author of the poetry collections *Acid Western* (The Operating System) and *Traces* (Ursus Americanus Press). His poems have appeared in *American Poetry Journal, Reality Beach, Powder Keg, TAGVVERK, Tammy, Prelude, Barrow Street, Apogee, Cosmonauts Avenue,* and others. He is also a union delegate for City College, and a PhD student in English at Stony Brook University.

WHY PRINT / DOCUMENT?

The Operating System uses the language "print document" to differentiate from the book-object as part of our mission to distinguish the act of documentation-in-book-FORM from the act of publishing as a backwards-facing replication of the book's agentive *role* as it may have appeared the last several centuries of its history. Ultimately, I approach the book as TECHNOLOGY: one of a variety of printed documents (in this case, bound) that humans have invented and in turn used to archive and disseminate ideas, beliefs, stories, and other evidence of production.

Ownership and use of printing presses and access to (or restriction of printed materials) has long been a site of struggle, related in many ways to revolutionary activity and the fight for civil rights and free speech all over the world. While (in many countries) the contemporary quotidian landscape has indeed drastically shifted in its access to platforms for sharing information and in the widespread ability to "publish" digitally, even with extremely limited resources, the importance of publication on physical media has not diminished. In fact, this may be the most critical time in recent history for activist groups, artists, and others to insist upon learning, establishing, and encouraging personal and community documentation practices. Hear me out.

With The OS's print endeavors I wanted to open up a conversation about this: the ultimately radical, transgressive act of creating PRINT /DOCUMENTATION in the digital age. It's a question of the archive, and of history: who gets to tell the story, and what evidence of our life, our behaviors, our experiences are we leaving behind? We can know little to nothing about the future into which we're leaving an unprecedentedly digital document trail — but we can be assured that publications, government agencies, museums, schools, and other institutional powers that be will continue to leave BOTH a digital and print version of their production for the official record. Will we?

As a (rogue) anthropologist and long time academic, I can easily pull up many accounts about how lives, behaviors, experiences — how THE STORY of a time or place — was pieced together using the deep study of correspondence, notebooks, and other physical documents which are no longer the norm in many lives and practices. As we move our creative behaviors towards digital note taking, and even audio and video, what can we predict about future technology that is in any way assuring that our stories will be accurately told – or told at all? How will we leave these things for the record?

In these documents we say:
WE WERE HERE, WE EXISTED, WE HAVE A DIFFERENT STORY

- Elæ [Lynne DeSilva-Johnson], Founder/Creative Director
THE OPERATING SYSTEM, Brooklyn NY 2018

RECENT & FORTHCOMING
OS PRINT::DOCUMENTS and PROJECTS, 2019-21

2020-21

Institution is a Verb: A Panoply Performance Lab Compilation
Vidhu Aggarwal - Daughter Isotope
Johnny Damm - Failure Biographies
Power ON - Ginger Ko
Spite - Danielle Pafunda
Acid Western - Robert Balun

KIN(D)* TEXTS AND PROJECTS

Intergalactic Travels: Poems from a Fugutive Alien - Alan Pelaez Lopez
HOAX - Joey De Jesus [Kin(d)*]
RoseSunWater - Angel Dominguez [Kin(d)*/Glossarium]
Bodies of Work - Elæ Moss & Georgia Elrod

GLOSSARIUM: UNSILENCED TEXTS AND TRANSLATIONS

Between Language and Justice: Selected Writings from Antena Aire
(Jen Hofer & John Pluecker))
Steven Alvarez - Manhatitlán [Glossarium]
Híkurí (Peyote) - José Vincente Anaya (tr. Joshua Pollock)
Ernst Toller's "Vormorgen" & Emmy Hennings - Radical Archival Translations -
Mathilda Cullen [Glossarium x Kin(d)*; German-English]
Black and Blue Partition ('Mistry) - Monchoachi (tr. Patricia Hartland)
[Glossarium; French & Antillean Creole/English]

IN CORPORE SANO

Hypermobilities - Ellen Samuels
Goodbye Wolf - Nik DeDominic

2019

Ark Hive-Marthe Reed
I Made for You a New Machine and All it Does is Hope - Richard Lucyshyn
Illusory Borders-Heidi Reszies
A Year of Misreading the Wildcats - Orchid Tierney
Of Color: Poets' Ways of Making | An Anthology of Essays on
Transformative Poetics - Amanda Galvan Huynh & Luisa A. Igloria, Editors

KIN(D)* TEXTS AND PROJECTS

A Bony Framework for the Tangible Universe-D. Allen [In Corpore Sano]
Opera on TV-James Brunton
Hall of Waters-Berry Grass
Transitional Object-Adrian Silbernagel

GLOSSARIUM: UNSILENCED TEXTS AND TRANSLATIONS

Śnienie / Dreaming - Marta Zelwan/Krystyna Sakowicz,
(Poland, trans. Victoria Miluch)
High Tide Of The Eyes - Bijan Elahi (Farsi-English/dual-language)
trans. Rebecca Ruth Gould and Kayvan Tahmasebian
In the Drying Shed of Souls: Poetry from Cuba's Generation Zero
Katherine Hedeen and Víctor Rodríguez Núñez, translators/editors
Street Gloss - Brent Armendinger with translations of Alejandro Méndez,
Mercedes Roffé, Fabián Casas, Diana Bellessi
& Néstor Perlongher (Argentina)
Operation on a Malignant Body - Sergio Loo
(Mexico, trans. Will Stockton)[In Corpore Sano]
Are There Copper Pipes in Heaven - Katrin Ottarsdóttir
(Faroe Islands, trans. Matthew Landrum)

DOC U MENT
/däkyəmənt/

First meant "instruction" or "evidence," whether written or not.

noun - a piece of written, printed, or electronic matter that provides information or evidence or that serves as an official record
verb - record (something) in written, photographic, or other form
synonyms - paper - deed - record - writing - act - instrument

[Middle English, precept, from Old French, from Latin *documentum*, example, proof, from *docre*, to teach; see *dek-* in Indo-European roots.]

Who is responsible for the manufacture of value?

Based on what supercilious ontology have we landed in a space where we vie against other creative people in vain pursuit of the fleeting credibilities of the scarcity economy, rather than freely collaborating and sharing openly with each other in ecstatic celebration of MAKING?

While we understand and acknowledge the economic pressures and fear-mongering that threatens to dominate and crush the creative impulse, we also believe that
now more than ever we have the tools to relinquish agency via cooperative means,
fueled by the fires of the Open Source Movement.

Looking out across the invisible vistas of that rhizomatic parallel country we can begin to see our community beyond constraints, in the place where intention meets resilient, proactive, collaborative organization.

Here is a document born of that belief, sown purely of imagination and will. When we document we assert. We print to make real, to reify our being there. When we do so with mindful intention to address our process, to open our work to others, to create beauty in words in space, to respect and acknowledge the strength of the page we now hold physical, a thing in our hand, we remind ourselves that, like Dorothy: *we had the power all along, my dears.*

THE PRINT! DOCUMENT SERIES
is a project of
the trouble with bartleby
in collaboration with
the operating system